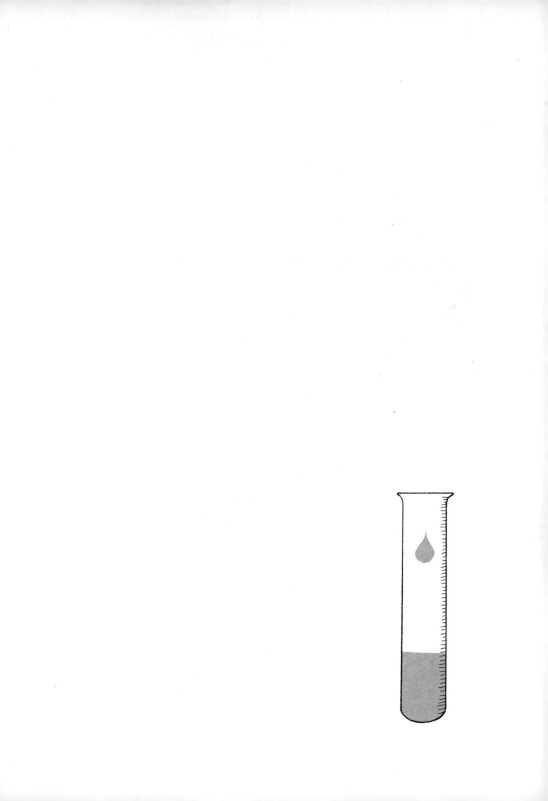

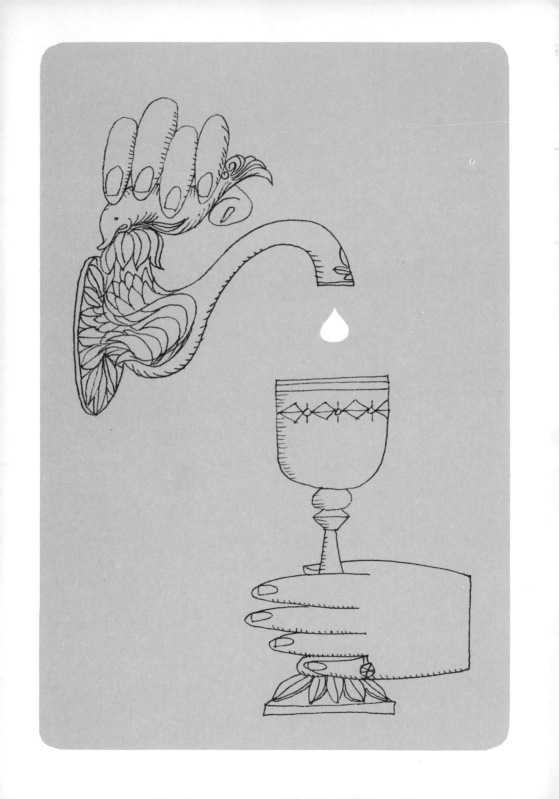

Drop by Drop:

A LOOK AT WATER

by A. Harris Stone
and Dale Ingmanson

ILLUSTRATED BY PETER P. PLASENCIA

PRENTICE-HALL, INC. • ENGLEWOOD CLIFFS, N.J.

For Fay and Irv

DROP BY DROP: A Look at Water
by A. Harris Stone and Dale Ingmanson

© 1969 by A. Harris Stone and Dale Ingmanson

Library of Congress Catalog Card Number: 69-10339
Printed in the United States of America • *J*

Prentice-Hall International, Inc., *London*
Prentice-Hall of Australia, Pty. Ltd., *Sydney*
Prentice-Hall of Canada, Ltd., *Toronto*
Prentice-Hall of India Private Ltd., *New Delhi*
Prentice-Hall of Japan, Inc., *Tokyo*

CONTENTS

INTRODUCTION

No matter what field of study a scientist is interested in, he needs to know a great deal about water. In fact, water may be the most commonly studied substance in the universe. The biologist needs to know as much as possible about water because it is the basic material of all plants and animals. Chemists study water because it is the most common liquid in which other substances can be dissolved. Geologists study the action of water on rocks and soil, while oceanographers investigate almost every idea about water that can possibly be studied.

Because of its importance to every person, water is an interesting subject for study by young scientists. In this book there are many questions about water. To answer these questions, you should try the experiments. Try each one in your own way. Do things as you think they should be done. And, ask more questions!

7

DISPLACEMENT: PUSHED AWAY!

When you blow through a straw into water, the bubbles that form always "disappear" in a few moments. Where do the bubbles go? What happens when a bottle full of water is held upside-down in a tank of water, just above the end of a bubble-making straw?

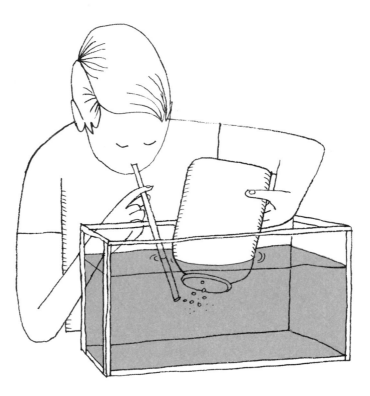

Do the bubbles "disappear"? Do any bubbles go down? Is the water level in the tank the same before and after the bubbles are made? Are the bubbles solid, liquid, gas or some other form?

By carefully observing bubbles as they move through liquids, scientists have discovered many ways in which water is different from other substances. The observations that have been made include measurements of how fast the bubbles move, how large they are, and what the bubbles do when they reach the surface. Is it possible to change the size or the speed of bubbles in water? Does the size of the straw have any effect on the bubble size or speed?

Biologists who wish to know how fast a plant releases a gas, such as oxygen, have often found answers by counting the bubbles that come from a water plant. The method they use is rather simple. Starting with a plant like *elodea,* they place it upside down in a test tube full of water. Then they shine a bright light on the plant and count the bubbles.

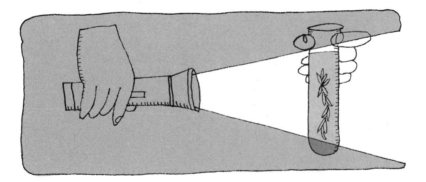

Does the age of the elodea have any effect on the production of bubbles? What happens when brighter light is used? A duller light?

Do bubbles form around people when they are taking a bath?

COMPOSITION: WHAT'S IT MADE OF?

How can a scientist find out what water is made of? What happens when an electric current passes through water? Do the bubbles form in each of the tubes at the same speed? Does anything happen when a little salt or vinegar is added to the water?

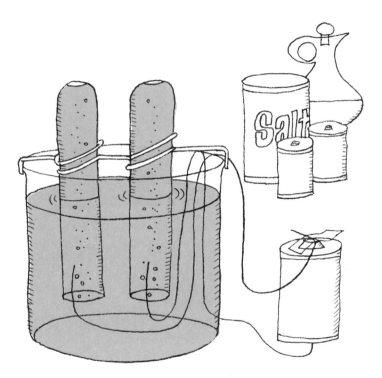

What happens when several batteries are used instead of one? What happens if both wires are placed inside one tube? How many more bubbles are collected in one tube than the other?

Where did the bubbles come from and what made them? These are the questions that scientists first asked when they watched the experiment of passing electricity through water. They also wondered what the bubbles were made of. Do both tubes have the same material in them? Do either of the tubes contain something that will burn? Try lighting the tube that has collected the largest number of bubbles. *Ask an adult to help with this!* If the substance in the tube burns, how can you find out what it is? Are there any other colorless gasses that burn? Does the gas in the other tube burn? Blow out a match and quickly push it into the tube that has collected the smaller amount of gas. What happens? How can you find out what gas is in the tube?

When a scientist has gathered all the information he possibly can from this experiment, he still does not have any answers. He usually refers to many books and other sources of reference to help him think about what he has seen. Then he proposes a possible explanation to the problem he is studying. In this experiment the problem may be thought of as "What is water made of?" Propose an answer to this problem by using both the information you gathered and reference books.

LIGHT TRANSMISSION: LIGHT GOES THROUGH!

When looking at an object, we usually think that "nothing" is between us and that object. Is it possible that there is something between the eyes and an object that the eyes are focused on? How does a wall or a window affect what we see? What happens to the image of what is seen when a tank of water is placed between the object and the eyes?

Does the object look different if the water is stirred? Add vegetable coloring to see if there is any change in what is seen. If a flash light is directed toward the tank, can any light be seen on the other side?

When an object can be seen clearly through a substance, that substance is called *transparent*. Most glass, many plastics and some other materials are transparent. Pure water that has not been stirred is usually similar to clear glass in the sense that objects may be seen through it. Most water found in nature does not fit the description of being *pure* and undisturbed. Can objects at the bottom of a rushing stream be seen clearly? Can they be seen at all? Does it matter how deep the stream is? Can objects be seen through ocean water? When viewing a sunken object in ocean water, what effect does the salt have?

Can the date on a coin be read if the coin is placed in a tall container of water?

What happens when trying to read the date if salt is added to the water? Sugar? If the water is stirred?

DENSITY: HOW HEAVY?

A steel ball will sink if it is dropped into water but steel ocean liners float. Will water sink if a teaspoon of it is dropped into a glass of oil? Does frozen water sink if placed in a glass of liquid water? How about in a glass of oil or vinegar?

When an ice cube floats, does it change the level of water in the glass? Does the water level go up as the ice melts? Does an ice cube float higher in salt water than in plain water?

It seems strange that one object can float while another object made of the same material will sink. Try floating an ice cube in a glass of rubbing alcohol. Mix rubbing alcohol with water and try again. What happens? Is there a difference when the mixture is more water than alcohol as compared to more alcohol than water?

If a solid ice cube floats in some liquids but not in others, the difference may be in the liquids. To find out, freeze water in various shapes and try to float each one in different liquids. Does the shape make any difference? Try making an ice cube that is cup-shaped by placing a ball in a container of water and then freezing it. Remove the ball from the ice before floating it. Does the cup-shaped ice float in any liquids in which solid shapes of ice sink?

VISCOSITY: HOW GOOEY?

Which takes longer to empty, a full glass of cold fruit juice or a glass of cold chocolate syrup? How much longer does one take than the other? Does vegetable oil run through a funnel faster or slower than water? Can the difference in time be measured?

Must equal amounts of water and oil be used when measuring the "run-through" time? Is there a difference in "run through" if a single piece of paper tissue is used to cover the inside of the funnel?

Not all liquids "run" at the same speed. Molasses runs at a much different speed than alcohol. To describe the difference in the speeds at which liquids pour, scientists use the word *viscosity*. The more slowly a liquid runs the more *viscose* they say it is. There are many factors which can change the viscosity of any liquid. Temperature can be one of these factors. Does chocolate syrup pour faster when it is cold or when it is warm? Another factor of viscosity is the presence of other substances dissolved or mixed into a liquid. Which pours faster— pure water? water with a lot of sugar dissolved in it? or water with some dirt mixed in? Does it matter how much sugar or how much dirt is used?

When scientists wish to know how viscose a liquid is, they do not have to measure the speed at which it pours. There are several other methods. One method is to find out how long it takes a small steel ball to fall from the top of a container of liquid to the bottom. Try this, using several liquids such as detergent, water, alcohol, vegetable oil and molasses.

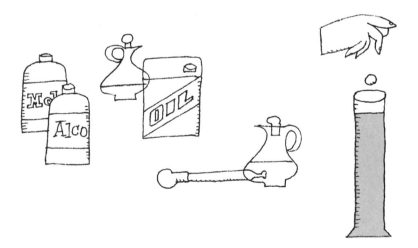

Try changing the temperatures of the liquids. Does the viscosity change?

VOLUME CHANGE: IT GETS BIGGER!

What happens to a glass jar filled with water when it is placed in the freezer for a day? *For safety, put the jar of water inside a plastic bag before placing it in the cold.* Will the same thing happen if a plastic bottle is used? Does it matter if the jar is full rather than almost full?

Try this again using alcohol or oil in place of water. Will the same thing happen if salt is added to the water before it is placed in the freezer?

18

People who live in the northern sections of the United States have learned about the effects of frozen water. One thing they are sure to do before winter is to put anti-freeze in the cooling system of their cars. They also drain any pipes that will not be warmed all winter by the heating system in their homes. They do these things because of what happens to water when it freezes. What happens is the same as what happened when you placed the jar of water in the freezer. Does water change in all ways when it becomes frozen? Try weighing a container of water before and after it is frozen. Has the weight changed?

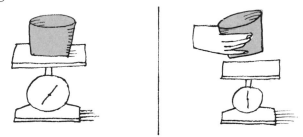

Measure around the outside of the plastic bottle of water before it is frozen. Measure around it again after freezing. Has the size changed?

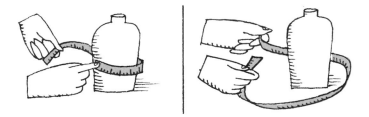

Does adding salt or sugar to the water change the weight or measurements taken around the outside of the bottle?

FREEZING POINT: HOW COLD?

Can water freeze at any temperature or does it become solid at one certain temperature? This question can be studied by reading a thermometer in water as shown here. The outside container has "dry ice" in it. *Be careful not to touch the dry ice with your hands! It produces severe injury to the skin.*

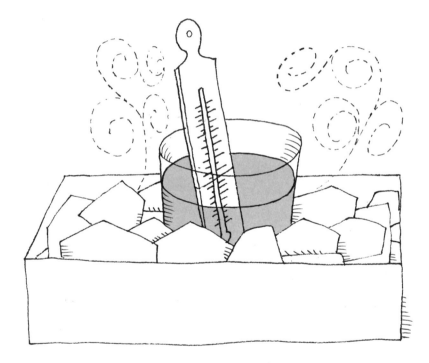

What temperature does the thermometer record when the water changes to ice? How often must you read the thermometer to answer that question? Why is dry ice used?

All liquids will become solids if the temperature is low enough. Some liquids, such as nitrogen, must be cooled hundreds of degrees before they solidify. Pure water has a temperature at which it freezes. Is this temperature always the same? Does the freezing temperature of water change if salt is added to the water? Does adding twice as much salt have any effect?

What happens to the temperature of water *as ice is forming?* Try stirring the water with a thermometer as ice forms. Does the water get colder during the time the ice is forming?

The ice formed by nature has a great effect on the climates of the world. Would you find it strange to see icebergs floating near the equator? Do you think swimming might be fun near the north pole?

BOILING POINT: HOW HOT?

Ask an adult to help you with this experiment!

Can a piece of steel be heated to 300°F. by placing it in boiling water? Does an uncovered pan of boiling water reach temperatures this high? To find out, read a thermometer placed in a pan of water that is being heated. At what temperature does the water boil?

If you do this five times, does the water always boil at the same reading on the thermometer? Does water from a stream, river or pond, boil at the same temperature as water from a faucet?

22

The temperature at which a liquid bubbles is called its boiling point. Every liquid has such a point; in fact, every liquid will boil. The boiling temperature is different for each liquid. By the same method as used with water, find the boiling point of vinegar. Is it close to that of water? What is vinegar made of?

The boiling points of liquids can be changed in several ways. What happens to the temperature at which water boils if a large amount of salt is added to the water before it is heated?

Another way of changing the boiling point of a liquid is to heat the liquid in a covered pot. How can the temperature inside the pot be read if the pot is covered during the time it is being heated? A pressure cooker is a closed pot. Does the temperature of water inside a pressure cooker get higher than that of water in an open pot?

EXPANSION

What happens to the water level in a narrow tube when the water temperature is increased? *Ask an adult to help you with this.*

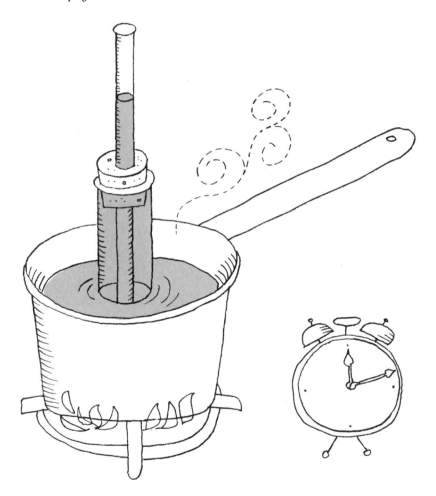

Does decreasing the temperature have an opposite effect?

How much water was in the tube before heating? Did the amount of water change? Did the level change? How far did the water level rise or fall? Can the exact percentage of level change be calculated? Suppose the change that occurred during heating was equal to 10% of the total volume of water in the test tube and in the narrow tube. Do your observations and your sense of logic support an estimate of 10% volume increase?

The oceans of the world contain about 300,000,000 cubic miles of water! Heat from the sun raises the temperature of ocean water. What would happen to the sea level if the temperature of all the oceans increased 20 degrees Fahrenheit?

The reaction of water to heating has several important effects. To illustrate one of these, think about this problem. A swimming pool is 50 feet long, 20 feet wide and 10 feet deep. It is filled with water to a depth of 9.8 feet. What will happen if the rise in water temperature causes a 2% expansion?

REFRACTION: IT LOOKS DIFFERENT!

Is there anything about a pencil resting in a glass half-full of water that looks different? Does the position of the pencil in water affect what is seen? Does the direction from which the pencil is viewed make any difference?

Is there any point from which the pencil appears to be in two pieces? Does the temperature of the water have any effect on what is seen?

The pencil that is placed in water is in two different materials at the same time. The top of the pencil is in air, the bottom in water. Can the same effects be seen if the entire pencil is submerged in water?

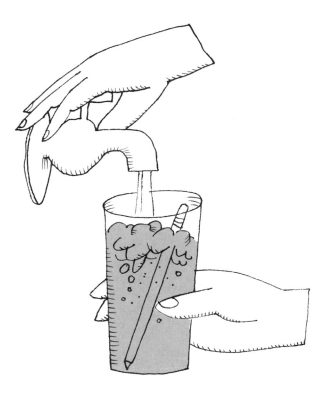

Does the shape of the container make any difference? Try putting a pencil in a container half-full that is square instead of round. Can anything different be seen? Is there any place from which the pencil in the square container can be viewed so that the pencil looks the same as it did in the round container?

MAGNIFICATION: IT LOOKS DIFFERENT!

Does a flat piece of glass placed on a piece of newspaper have any effect on the newsprint seen through the glass? Does waxed paper used in place of glass have any effect? Can anything different be seen if a drop of water is placed on the glass or on the waxed paper?

Are the letters on the newspaper clear? What has happened to the size of the letters that can be seen through the drop of water?

When viewing letters on newsprint through a drop of water, it is helpful to compare what is seen when not looking through the drop. Do the letters have the same appearance when seen through a very large drop as when seen through a small one? What is the shape of the small drop? The large one? Use vegetable oil in place of water to see if there is a difference. Does the temperature of the water or oil make any difference? Does the depth of the water change what is seen?

The curvature of the drop is related to the change that can be seen. This change can also be seen when using pieces of glass that have the same shape. Compare the effect seen when a lens is placed on the newsprint with the effect of the water drop.

ADHESION: IT STICKS!

What happens to a piece of wet paper when it is placed on a window? How long will the paper stay in the position it is placed in? Does the temperature of the water or the window have any effect on how long it stays?

Will a piece of paper coated with a thin film of oil do the same as paper and water? Will vinegar work the same way?

When any substance sticks to another substance we can think of the two substances as being "glued" to each other. When the two substances are different from each other, the sticking together is called *adhesion*. The sticking power of *adhesion* depends on the kinds of substances that are placed together. It would be hard to imagine a tape with water on it being used to fasten a piece of paper to a window. Even though the water would work, what would happen when the water dried out? Does the sticky substance on one side of cellophane tape every dry out? What is the substance that is usually used on cellophane tape?

The strength of *adhesion* can be measured to find out what materials *adhere* best. By wetting two pieces of glass with a liquid like water the adhesive value of the water can be determined. The amount of force needed to pull the two pieces of glass apart shows how much the water makes them stick together. Is oil more or less adhesive than water?

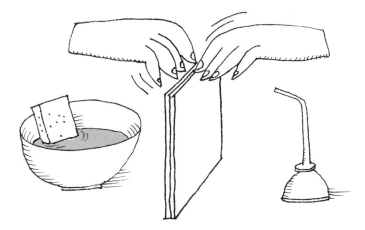

HEAT RETENTION: IT'S STILL HOT!

How long does it take for a pot of water to cool from the boiling temperature to room temperature? Does it take half as long to cool to half the temperature between boiling and room temperature? How long does it take to heat water from room temperature to the boiling temperature?

Does it matter what the room temperature is on the day this is done? When water is cooling, does it matter what kind of surface the pot is placed on? Does water cool as fast when a cover is placed on the pot?

Air temperature and climate in cities near the ocean are different from the temperature and climate inland. Will a sun lamp change the temperature of water in a glass? Will the same thing happen if the water is replaced with soil or sand?

Does soil cool faster than water?

Different substances retain different amounts of heat. If the substance is a large body of water, like a lake or ocean, air temperature and climate will be affected. What effect do volcanoes and geysers have on temperature and climate?

REGELATION: IT'S STILL ONE!

How can one solid pass through another without either material ending up in two pieces? When an axe passes through a piece of wood, the wood becomes two pieces. What happens when a weighted wire is placed across a piece of ice?

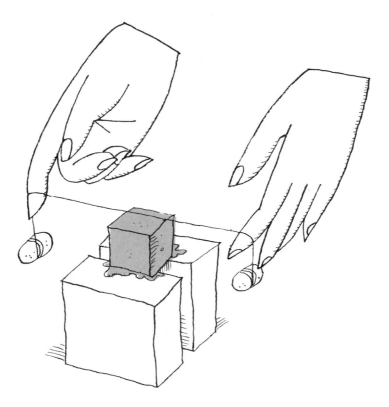

Be patient, this may take some time. Does it matter how thick the wire is? It may be less messy if some paper towels are placed under the ice cube at the beginning.

The observations, during the time of this experiment, usually lead to interesting questions. How can the wire do what it does? What happened to the ice cube? The ice cube in this experiment is a good example of things happening that are not expected. When a scientist finds himself in this situation he usually tries to decide what is going on by doing another experiment. In this case there are three items that can be studied: the ice cube, the wire and the weights. Through a study of any one of these, he *may* find out what is going on in the process which has been named *regelation*.

As an example of how a scientist might study one of the items, consider what questions can be asked of the weights. Does the kind of materials used for weights make any difference? Do their shapes matter? Does the same thing happen if the weights pull at an angle? What happens if the weights are heavier? lighter? Does what happens take less time or more time with heavier weights?

By the time the scientist has asked and answered these questions about the weights, he will also know a great deal about the wire and the ice cube. He will know about these because when studying questions about weights, he must experiment not only with them but with the wire and ice as well.

What made what happened happen?

BUOYANCY: IT FLOATS!

How much of a floating block of wood is above water? Does this amount change if a block is hollow? What happens to the water level on the block if nails or screws are placed in the block? Do more nails show a larger effect?

What is the difference when alcohol or oil is used in place of water? When a steel or aluminum block is used in place of the wooden one?

An object that floats in water or in any other liquid is called a *buoyant* object. *Buoyancy* is a term used to describe the quality of flotation. Most people think of objects floating in water, but you have just observed an object floating in another liquid. What difference is there between an object's buoyancy in water and its buoyancy in another liquid? What happens if water is placed on top of oil? Is this different than what happens when water is placed on top of the liquid called mercury? Is water buoyant in either oil or mercury? What happens when oil is placed in water?

So far we have considered only the buoyancy of solid objects in liquids and liquids in liquids. Can solids be buoyant in other solids? What happens when a piece of metal is placed in a jar full of flour or on a block of wood? Is flour a solid, a liquid or something else?

What happens when a metal ball is placed on a mound of Silly Putty?

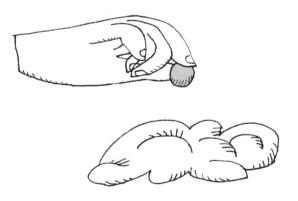

Does a wooden ball act the same way as a metal ball would when placed on Silly Putty? What happens if the Silly Putty is made warmer or colder?

37

LUBRICATION: IT'S SLIPPERY!

A lump of clay placed on a board will rest where it is placed until something moves it. What happens if the clay is placed on a slanted board? How slanted must the board be before something happens? Does a board that is wet have to be more or less slanted in order for something to happen?

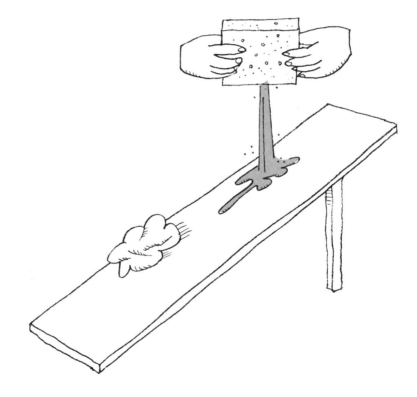

Will oil act the same way water does? Does a block of wood used in place of clay do what the clay does on a water-wet board? On an oiled board?

A *lubricant* is a material which allows two objects to slide across each other more easily than they would if the lubricant were not used. Most people think of oil when they have need for a lubricant. Oil is used in many places to permit a free-movement of objects. It is used on cars to help them work more easily and to make door-hinges swing more freely. Water can also work as a lubricant and often does just that in man's natural world. Have you ever seen pictures of mud slides? Mud slides occur when earth gets soaked with water and the particles of earth start sliding over one another. Do mud slides happen on level places? How steep must a slope be before mud will slide? How can you find out how steep the slope must be?

Does it make any difference how much water is mixed with the earth?

MIXING LIQUIDS

How many pints of mixture will result from adding one pint of water to one pint of vinegar? Is there any difference if one pint of water is added to one pint of alcohol? Try this—you'll be amazed!

Is there a different result if cold water and cold alcohol are used? Is there any change in volume if the mixture is stirred?

The effect that is seen when alcohol and water are mixed is the kind of observation that causes scientists to ask, "What is responsible for the effect that I see?" Sometimes they can study the question directly by doing similar experiments and trying to relate the results of the new experiments to the questions of the original one. Similar experiments are not often easy to do. Then scientists study the problems indirectly by using models of the original experiment. You can try both the direct and indirect approach to find out what happened when alcohol and water were mixed.

Can any change be noticed if water colored with vegetable dye is added to alcohol? Does the shape of the container have any effect on what is seen?

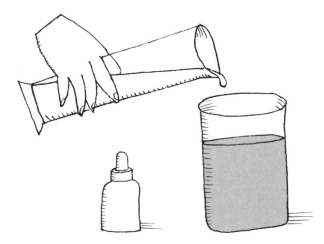

What happens when a container of sand is added to an equal size container of marbles? If the sand and marbles are poured into a container that is twice as large as either the container of marbles or the one of sand, does the larger container become full?

WATER-MOVEMENT AND TEMPERATURE

What happens to a drop of vegetable dye when it is gently placed in a jar of still, cold water? What happens when the water is gently stirred? When it is stirred vigorously? Is there any difference when hot water is used in place of cold water?

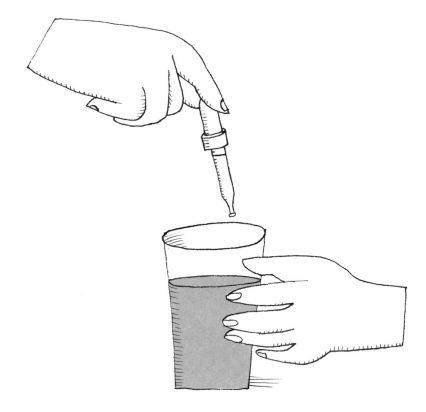

Does the same thing happen when dyes of different colors are used? Does the kind of container make any difference?

The effect that is seen when a drop of dye or coloring is placed in a liquid depends on several different conditions. You have probably noticed the different effects in experiments when hot water is used in place of cold water. What difference is there between using hot or cold dye? Another important difference in what is observed can be seen by using various liquids. Does the drop move differently in oil than it does in water? What happens when alcohol is used?

The mixing of water with another liquid is dependent on many factors. Two that you have seen so far are the temperature and the nature of the other liquid. Still another factor that can be studied concerns what is dissolved in the liquid that is mixing. What happens when vegetable coloring is added to a strong salt solution?

IMBIBITION

What effect does water have on dried seeds that are soaked in water for several hours? Do the seeds feel different after soaking? What happens to a tightly-capped jar of dried lima beans and water? Be patient, this may take a whole day! *Be careful when removing the cap—it may be dangerous!*

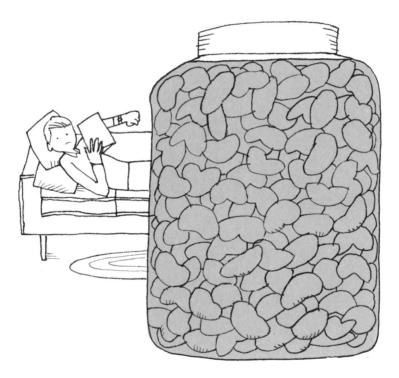

Can a different effect be seen if hot water is used instead of cool water? Does dry corn work the same way lima beans do?

The effect that is observed when dry seeds are soaked in water is called *imbibition*. The *imbibition* effect is dependent on the beans soaking up the water. An interesting study of imbibition can be made by measuring the temperature of the beans soaking in water. Does the temperature change when different kinds of seeds are used?

What effect does adding salt have on the temperature readings? Can alcohol be used instead of water?

DISTORTION

Is a penny always seen in the bottom of a glass container filled with water? How about a dime? Does the shape of the container have any effect on whether the coin can be seen? Can the coin be seen from all angles?

Does the temperature of the water make any difference? Will the same effect be seen if oil is used instead of water? Does the color of the glass container have any effect on the ability to see the coin?

When objects are submerged in liquids, the light reflected from them is not the same as that reflected from objects out of liquids. Light moving through a medium such as air or water is affected by the medium. Since substances in air are spaced farther apart than substances in water, light is affected less by air than by water.

Some light hits a substance and bounces back. This produces a reflection. Some light bends as it passes through a substance. This bending or wavering is called *distortion*.

Will more distortion occur in moving water than in still water?

47

PARTICLE REFLECTION

Does water reflect light? How does mixing dirt with water affect the passage of light through the water? Does light passing through a sugar solution act in the same way as light passing through a mixture of flour and water? What effect is noticed when only a little flour is used? A lot of flour?

Does the brightness of the light make any difference? What difference is there if the experiment is repeated in a dark room with the flashlight as the only source of light?

The difference between sugar mixed with water, and dirt mixed with water is apparent when the two mixtures are observed. What happens to sugar *as* it is being stirred into water? When substances do what sugar does *as* it is being stirred into water, those substances are said to be dissolving. Does dirt dissolve? Do salt, pepper, baking soda, iron filings or sand dissolve in water? What happens to those substances which do not dissolve in water? Do all non-dissolving substances sink when placed in water?

Vegetable color, which is a dye, is frequently added to water. Does it dissolve? Sink? What can be seen when a flashlight is shined on a mixture of water and vegetable dye?

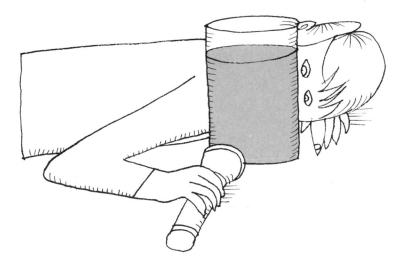

Do different color dyes cause different effects? What effect is seen if the light is shined on a mixture of dyes and dirt in water?

EVAPORATION

What happens to water that is boiled continuously? Where does it go? Is it still a liquid?

Do rain water, sea water, and river water react the same to heat as water from a faucet does? What happens when a small dish of water is left on a window sill for a few days? Does the water change in the same way it would if it were boiled?

The process of changing a liquid into a gas is called *evaporation*. How does the temperature of a liquid affect the speed of evaporation? Will water in a dish evaporate when put into a refrigerator?

Great Salt Lake in Utah used to be much larger than it is now. Old water marks on the mountains show that the lake was once very high. Slowly, evaporation and a lack of rain reduced the amount of water in the lake. As the water level continued to fall, the flat lake bottom was exposed. This lake bottom is now the famous Utah racing flats where automobile speed records are set.

DISTILLATION

How can a mixture of dirt and water be separated so that there is no dirt left in the water?

Is there any dirt left in the water after it flows through the funnel lined with cheese cloth? Is there as much dirt left if the water is passed through paper toweling?

Can sugar in water be separated from the water by the same method used to separate dirt from water? What happens to the sugar if the mixture of sugar and water is heated until it boils gently for about a half hour? Does the liquid in the pan taste sweet before the water is boiled?

Does the liquid in the pan taste sweet after it is boiled? Does it look the same after it is boiled as it did before boiling? Does the water in the cup taste sweet? *Ask an adult to help you with this one!*

CONDUCTIVITY

Can electricity be passed through pure water? What is *pure* water? How can you tell if electricity is passing through the water?

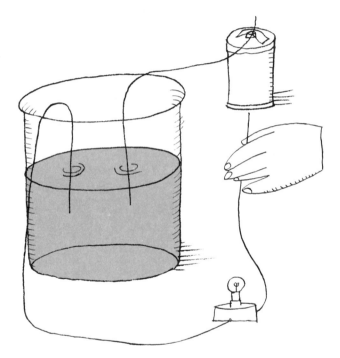

Does the strength of the battery or the size of the bulb have any effect on what happens?

Pure water is water only! It has *no* substance dissolved in it nor any particles suspended in it! Water coming from a faucet is not pure in the scientific sense of the word "pure." To make water pure, you must remove *all* other substances from it. To do this, the water can be boiled and the steam cooled. The cooled steam is almost pure water and if the process of boiling water and cooling steam is repeated several times, the final product is pure water. You have seen what happens when you try to pass electricity through pure water. Will electricity pass through water that has salt added to it? Sugar? Dirt? Pepper? Sand?

Does the amount of salt added have any effect on what the light bulb does? What other factors affect the light bulbs reaction?

ABSORPTION

How much does a dry sponge weigh? By using a balance or letter scale the weight of such an object can be found. How much does a sponge weigh after it has been soaked in water? What comparison can be made between the wet and the dry weight?

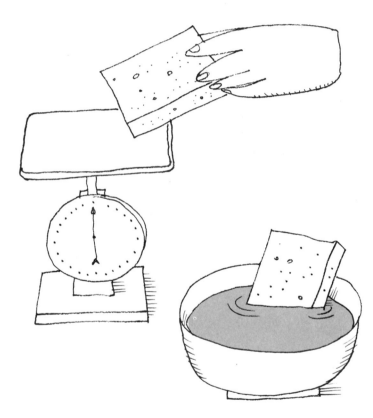

Will a block of wood the same size as the sponge absorb the same amount of water?

When water seeps into a substance, the substance is said to absorb water. Will water seep into any substance? Try blocks of metal, plastic, and other materials. Does the size or weight of a substance affect its ability to absorb water? What major characteristic of water makes absorption possible? Will oil or other liquids seep into substances?

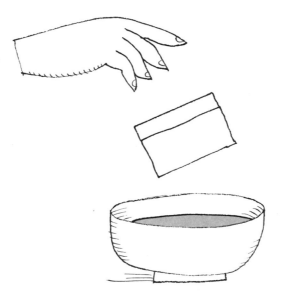

Many substances in the natural world absorb water. The ones that absorb water the most are used in garden soil in dry climates. Vermiculite is a substance that absorbs water and is used to hold water in soil. It can be bought at most garden centers and stores. Will an ounce of vermiculite absorb as much water as an ounce of sponge?

CAPILLARY ACTION

Do all kinds of paper absorb water? Will facial tissue absorb as much water as a piece of waxed paper? Will water move up different kinds of paper at the same speed?

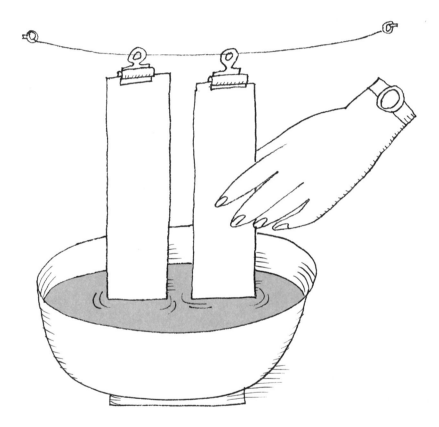

Does it make any difference how far the bottoms of the paper strips are placed under water? What kind of paper will absorb water the fastest?

Water can seep up in spite of gravity by a process called *capillary action*. Capillary action occurs when water is attracted by a substance. The exact cause of this attraction is not fully understood. To explore the cause, several experiments can be done. Will *pure water* move up a strip of paper by capillary action as far as tap water?

The process by which plants absorb water is of great importance to botanists. Will a plant that is watered from the top grow differently than a plant that gets its water from below?

GLOSSARY

ABSORPTION—A process by which one substance passes into another substance.

ADHESION—The condition of two unlike substances sticking together or resisting separation.

BOILING POINT—The temperature at which a liquid becomes a gas; it almost always is accompanied by the production of bubbles.

BUOYANCY—A condition of a floating substance when it is placed into another substance.

CAPILLARY ACTION—The action of a liquid rising through some material; the material through which the liquid rises has many small pores or tube-like structures called capillaries.

COMPOSITION—The individual parts which make up a substance.

CONDUCTIVITY—The ability of a substance to transfer heat, electricity, sound, or other types of energy through it.

CURVATURE—The condition of being rounded or the amount of roundness.

DENSITY—An expression of the amount of matter that is packed into a specified space or volume.

DISPLACEMENT—The process by which one substance takes the place of another substance.

DISSOLVE—To pass into a solution as sugar dissolves in water, forming a sugar-water solution.

DISTILLATION—The process of separating one substance from another by changing its form through heating; as water becomes steam when heated.

DRY ICE—Solid carbon dioxide.

ELODEA—A water plant that is often used in fish tanks.

EVAPORATION—The process of changing from a liquid to a gas.

EXPAND—To increase in volume or size.

FREEZING POINT—The temperature at which a liquid changes to a solid.

HEAT RETENTION—Maintaining a temperature in spite of a change in temperature of surrounding substances.

IMBIBITION—The process by which a liquid is taken in by another substance; it involves no chemical change in either substance.

LUBRICATION—The process by which the friction of a substance is reduced; it is usually accomplished by the addition of another substance, and the lubricant is the substance that is added.

MAGNIFICATION—The process of making a substance appear larger than it really is.

MIXTURE—A blend of two or more substances in which no chemical changes occur.

PURE WATER—Water with no dissolved substances or suspended particles in it.

REFLECTION—The orderly rebounding or bouncing back of light from a surface.

REFRACTION—A slight bending of a light beam usually caused by a change in the type of substance through which the light beam is traveling.

REGELATION—The process by which a solid, such as ice, melts and then solidifies; it is caused by an increase of pressure.

SOLUTION—The result of combining two or more substances in which a chemical change occurs producing a complex liquid.

TRANSPARENT—The quality of allowing light to pass through a material without being distorted so that an image can be seen.

VISCOSITY—A measure of the ability of a liquid to flow or to be poured.